KS1
5–7
Years

Master Maths at Home

Geometry and Shape

Scan the QR code to help your child's learning at home.

 MATHS
NO PROBLEM!

mastermathsathome.com

How to use this book

Maths — No Problem! created **Master Maths at Home** to help children develop fluency in the subject and a rich understanding of core concepts.

Key features of the Master Maths at Home books include:

- Carefully designed lessons that provide structure but also allow flexibility in how they're used. For example, some children may want to write numbers, while others might want to trace.

- Speech bubbles containing content designed to spark diverse conversations, with many discussion points that don't have obvious 'right' or 'wrong' answers.

- Rich illustrations that will guide children to a discussion of shapes and units of measurement, allowing them to make connections to the wider world around them.

- Exercises that allow a flexible approach and can be adapted to suit any child's cognitive or functional ability.

- Clearly laid out pages that encourage children to practise a range of higher-order skills.

- A community of friendly and relatable characters who introduce each lesson and come along as your child progresses through the series.

You can see more guidance on how to use these books at **mastermathsathome.com**.

We're excited to share all the ways you can learn maths!

Copyright © 2022 Maths — No Problem!

Maths — No Problem!
mastermathsathome.com
www.mathsnoproblem.com
hello@mathsnoproblem.com

First published in Great Britain in 2022 by
Dorling Kindersley Limited
One Embassy Gardens, 8 Viaduct Gardens, London SW11 7BW
A Penguin Random House Company

The authorised representative in the EEA is Dorling Kindersley
Verlag GmbH. Amulfstr. 124, 80636 Munich, Germany

10 9 8 7 6 5 4 3 2
003–327071–Jan/22

A CIP catalogue record for this book is available from the British Library.

ISBN: 978-0-24153-913-2
Printed and bound in the UK

For the curious
www.dk.com

This book was made with Forest Stewardship Council™ certified paper – one small step in DK's commitment to a sustainable future. For more information go to www.dk.com/our-green-pledge

MIX
Paper from responsible sources
FSC™ C018179

Acknowledgements
The publisher would like to thank the authors and consultants Andy Psarianos, Judy Hornigold, Adam Gifford and Dr Anne Hermanson.

The Castledown typeface has been used with permission from the Colophon Foundry.

Contents

Ruby   Elliott   Amira   Charles   Lulu   Sam   Oak   Holly   Ravi   Emma   Jacob   Hannah

Identifying sides

Starter

This is one **side** of a triangle.

How many sides do these shapes have?

Example

We can count the number of sides.

1 This is a triangle.

All triangles have 3 sides.

2 These are rectangles.

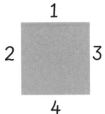

All rectangles have 4 sides.

1 Write the number of sides that each shape has.

(a)

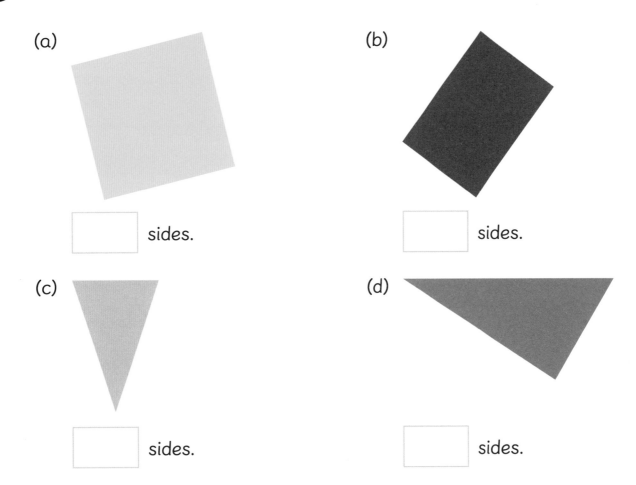

[   ] sides.

(b)

[   ] sides.

(c)

[   ] sides.

(d)

[   ] sides.

2 Circle the shapes with 4 sides.

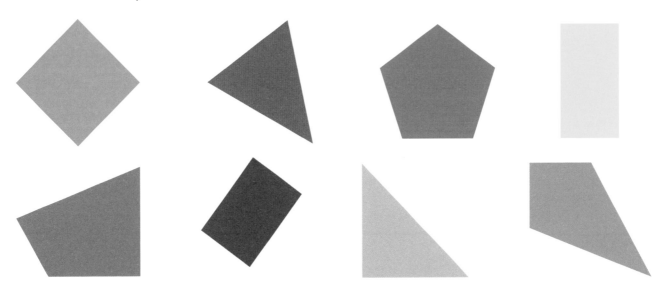

Identifying vertices

Starter

How can we sort these shapes?

Example

These shapes are all polygons.
All the sides of a polygon are
straight.

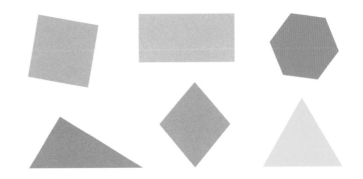

The point where two lines
meet is called a **vertex**.

The plural for
vertex is **vertices**.

These shapes are not polygons.
Not all of their sides are straight.

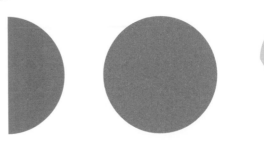

Circle the vertices on the shapes and complete the table.

	Polygon	Number of vertices	Number of sides
1			
2			
3			
4			
5			
6			
7			
8			

Identifying lines of symmetry

Starter

Can we fold these shapes so one half covers the other half exactly?

Example

When we fold the square like this, the two halves match exactly.

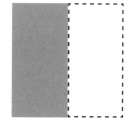

We can also fold the square like this because each half is the same.

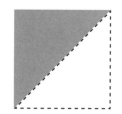

We say that a square is **symmetrical**.

←————— line of symmetry

The fold line is called the line of symmetry.

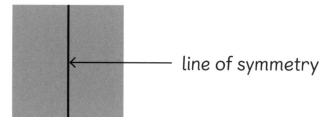

We can't fold this shape exactly in half. It does not have a line of symmetry.

Which of the following shapes are symmetrical?
Put a tick (✓) or cross (✗) next to each shape.

	Shape	Is it symmetrical?
1		
2		
3		
4		
5		
6		
7		
8		

Making figures

Starter

Is it possible to arrange 3 of these shapes to make a symmetrical figure?

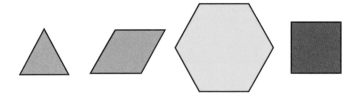

Example

I made this figure. It is not symmetrical. It does not have a line of symmetry.

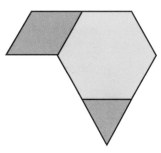

I made this figure. It is symmetrical. It has a line of symmetry.

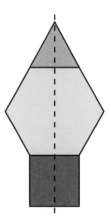

I made this figure. It is also symmetrical.

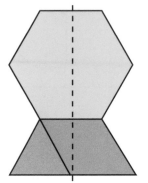

1 Draw two shapes that are symmetrical. Mark the line of symmetry on each shape.

2 Use  and

to make two figures, one that is symmetrical and one that is not symmetrical.

Draw them here.

3 Circle the shapes that are symmetrical and draw the lines of symmetry.

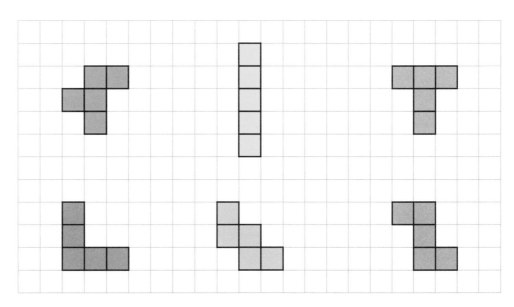

Sorting shapes

Starter

How can we sort these shapes?

Example

Polygons	Not polygons

I am looking for polygons.

3 straight sides	4 or more straight sides

I am looking at the number of straight sides.

Symmetrical	Not symmetrical

I am looking for symmetrical shapes.

Look at the shapes below.

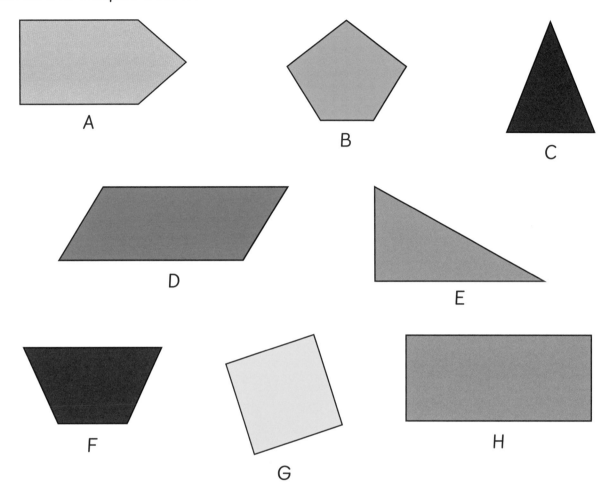

1 Sort the shapes by the number of vertices.

3 vertices	4 vertices	5 vertices

2 Sort the shapes by their lines of symmetry.

No line of symmetry	One line of symmetry	More than one line of symmetry

Drawing shapes

Starter

What shape can we draw?

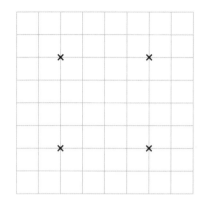

Example

Join up the crosses.

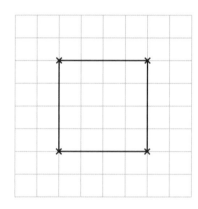

This shape has 4 straight sides and 4 vertices.
All the sides are the same length. It is a square.

We can draw other shapes as well.

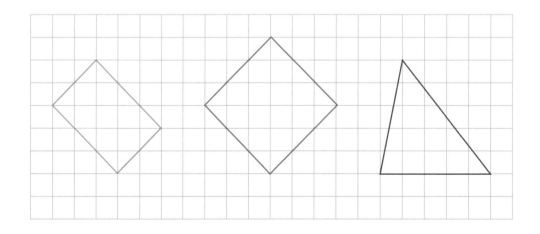

1 Copy these figures on the square grid below.

 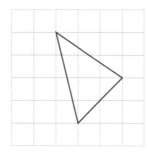 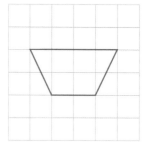

2 Draw a rectangle and a symmetrical triangle on the square grid below.

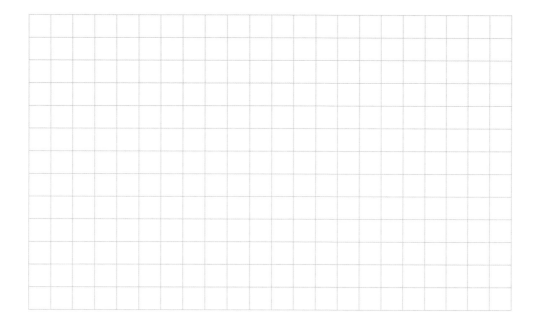

Making patterns (part 1)

Starter

What repeating patterns can we make with these shapes?

Example

1  made this pattern.

 made this pattern.

2 Here are some other repeating patterns.

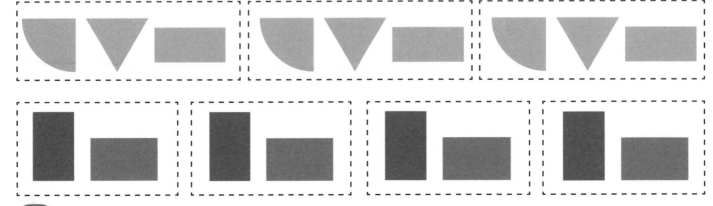

1 Make some repeating patterns using these shapes.

Draw your patterns here.

2 Draw the missing shapes in the boxes for each of these repeating patterns.

(a)

(b)

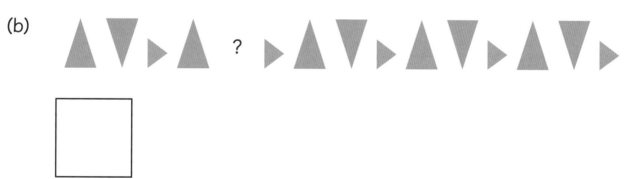

(c)

Describing patterns

Starter

How can we describe this pattern?

Example

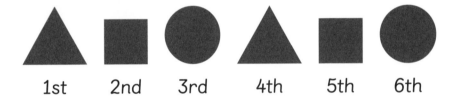

1st   2nd   3rd   4th   5th   6th

The pattern uses three different shapes.

The 1st shape is a blue triangle.

The 2nd shape is a blue square.

Every 3rd shape is a blue circle.

The 3rd shape is a blue circle.

Do you know what the 9th shape will be?
What about the 99th shape?

The 9th and 99th shapes will both be .

The 100th shape will start the pattern again. It will be a .

1 Draw the 12th shape in these patterns.

(a)

1st   ...

12th

(b)

1st   ...

12th

2 Draw the 1st shape in these patterns.

(a)

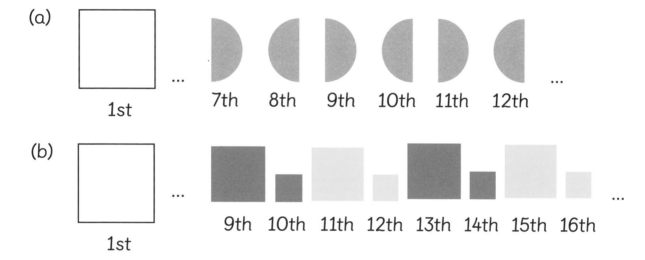

1st   ...   7th   8th   9th   10th   11th   12th   ...

(b)

1st   ...   9th   10th   11th   12th   13th   14th   15th   16th   ...

3 Make a pattern using these shapes.

Ask an adult if they can predict what the 10th shape will be.

Moving shapes

Describe how to move to triangle A and to triangle B.

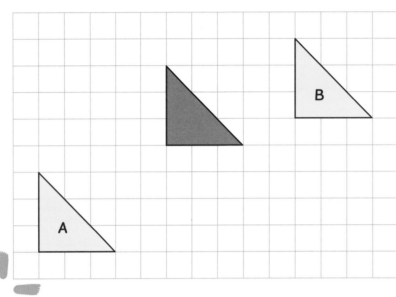

1 step

1 step

Example

 gave these instructions to move to triangle A.

Move 5 steps to the left.

Move 4 steps down.

> Does it matter in what order we make these movements?

 gave these instructions to move to triangle B.

Move 5 steps to the right.

Move 1 step up.

1 Draw the new position of each shape after moving each one 2 steps to the right and 1 step down.

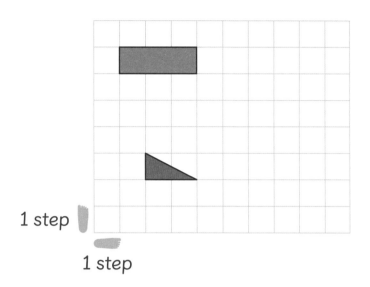

1 step

1 step

2 Draw the new position of each shape after moving each one 3 steps to the right and 2 steps up.

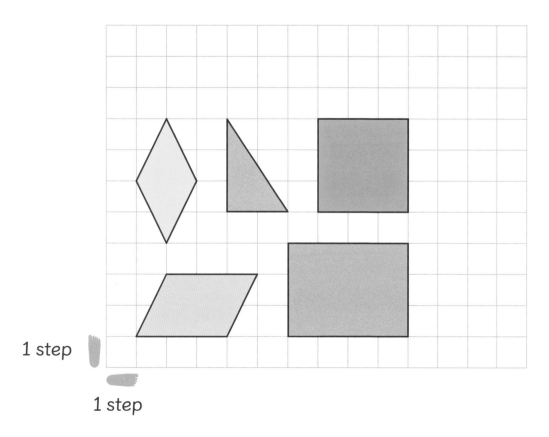

1 step

1 step

Turning shapes

What will be the new position of the
after a half turn clockwise?

Example

Turn ⬜ clockwise by half a turn.

We can also make quarter turns and three-quarter turns.

Turn ⬜ anticlockwise by
a quarter turn.

Turn ⬜ clockwise by
three-quarters of a turn.

1 Draw the new positions of ⮚ after:

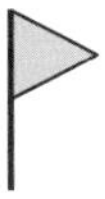

(a) a quarter turn clockwise

(b) a half turn anticlockwise.

2 Draw the new positions of  △ after:

(a) half a turn

(b) three-quarters of a turn anticlockwise.

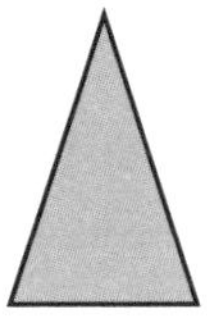

23

Solving word problems with 2D shapes

Starter

How many are needed to make 2 ?

Example

This is a circle.

This is a semi-circle.

This is a quarter circle.

When we put two together we make .

When we put two together we make .

4 make ⬤ .

For 2 circles we need 8 .

1 cuts a slice of cake like this.

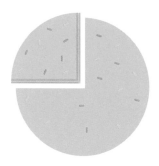

How many people can have a piece the same size as this?

 people can have a piece of cake.

2 What time will this clock show when the minute hand has moved a quarter circle from 12 to 3?

The clock will show .

3 Each friend will eat a of pizza.

How many friends will these pizzas serve?

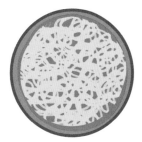

Recognising 3D shapes

Starter

What are the names of these shapes?

Example

This shape has a curved surface.
It is called a **sphere**.

A sphere can roll.
It has no flat sides.

This is a **cube**.
Each side is
a square.

This is a
cuboid.

These shapes have flat sides
and straight edges.

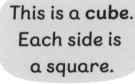

This shape has both flat and curved sides.
It is called a **cylinder**.

1. Match each shape to its name.

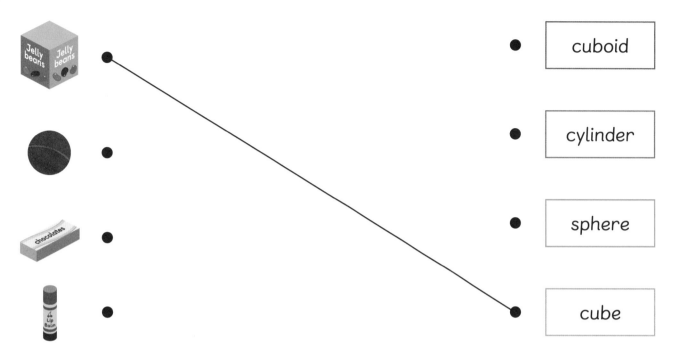

- cuboid
- cylinder
- sphere
- cube

2. Look around your home for different 3D shapes.
Record your findings in a table.

Item	Name of shape

3. Look at the sides of the shapes you find. Are they curved or flat?

Item	Curved	Flat

Describing 3D shapes

How can we describe these shapes?

This hat is shaped like a **cone**.
A cone has a flat face and a curved surface.

We call a flat side a **face**. We call a curved side a **surface**.

This box is shaped like a cuboid.
A cuboid has 6 faces.
The faces are rectangles.

This box is also a cuboid. The faces are squares and rectangles.

28

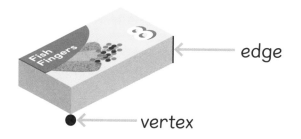

edge

vertex

It has 12 edges and 8 vertices.

Count the number of edges and vertices on a cuboid.

A cube is a special cuboid.
It has 6 faces. All the faces are squares.
It has 12 edges and 8 vertices.

This is a pyramid. It has 5 faces.
1 face is a square and the other 4 faces are triangles.

Can you describe the shape of this tent?
Look at the faces.
It is shaped like a prism.

A triangular prism has 9 edges and 6 vertices.

1 Match the objects with their shapes.

cuboid •

prism •

cube •

cylinder •

pyramid •

cone •

•

•

•

•

2 Describe each of the following shapes by completing the table.

Shape	Name	Number of faces	Number of vertices	Number of edges

3 What 3D shapes can you find in your home?
Record your findings in the table.

Item	Name	Number of faces	Number of vertices	Number of edges

Grouping 3D shapes

How can we group these shapes?

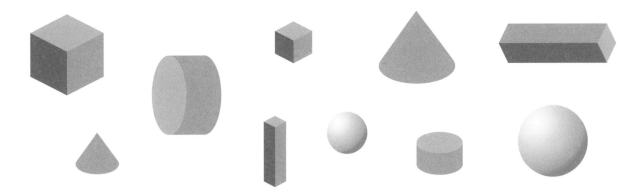

Example

We can group the shapes by the types of faces or surfaces they have.

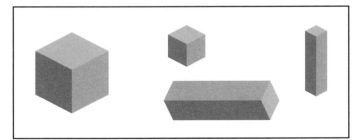 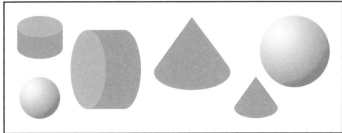

We can also group them by shape.

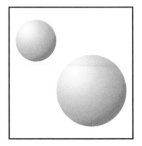 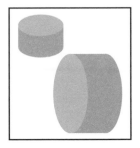  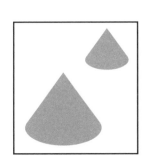 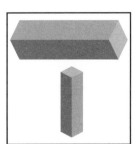

Match the objects with their shapes.

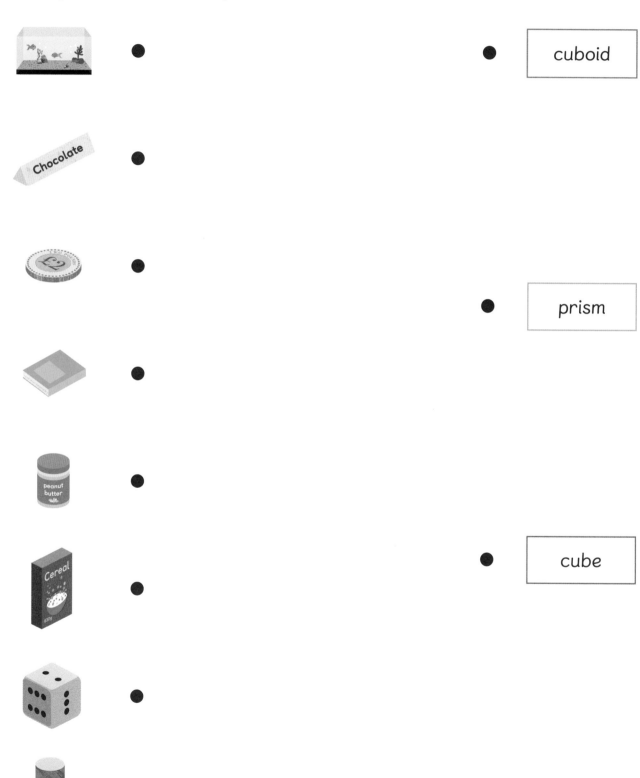

cuboid

prism

cube

cylinder

Forming 3D structures

What structures can we make using these shapes?

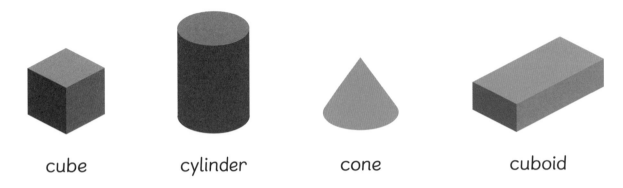

cube   cylinder   cone   cuboid

Example

I made this structure.

I made this structure.

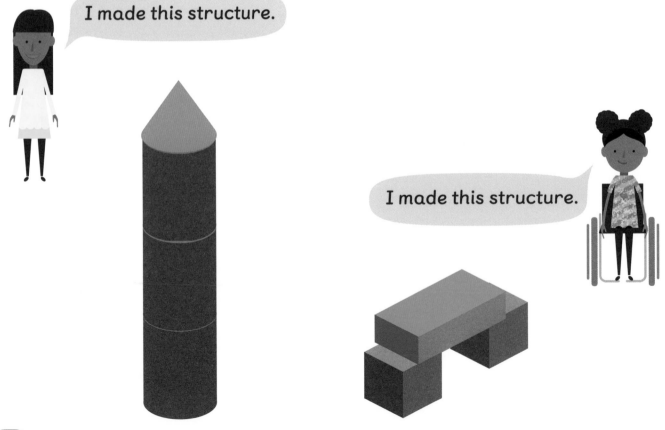

1 Look for 3D shapes in your home.
What shapes did you find?

2 Make different structures from the shapes. Cover one of them with a cloth. Describe it to a member of your family. Can they make one exactly the same from your description without seeing it?

If you have a set
of building blocks at home
you can use those.

Matching 3D shapes to 2D nets

Starter

Elliott unfolds a box to put into the recycling bin.
What shape will it make when it is flat?

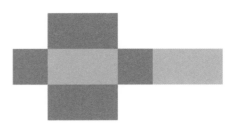

Example

 is a cuboid.

Elliott unfolds the cuboid.

 →

 is a cube.

Elliott unfolds the cube.

 →

 is a prism.

Elliott unfolds the prism.

 →

1 Match the nets to the 3D shapes.

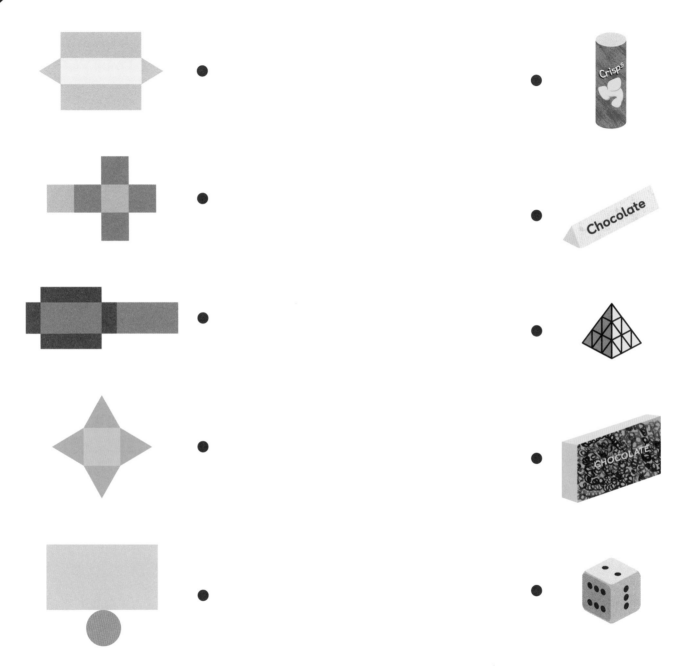

2 Find some boxes or cartons in your home and think about what their nets might look like.
Ask an adult to help you open up the boxes.

Making patterns (part 2)

Starter

What shape is missing from this pattern?

Example

The repeating pattern is 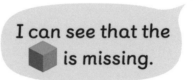.

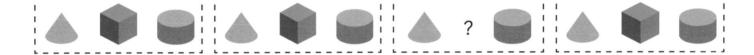

I can see that the is missing.

Practice

1 Circle the next shape in these patterns.

(a)

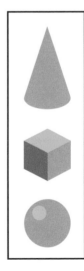

38

(b)

2 Circle the missing shape in these patterns.

(a)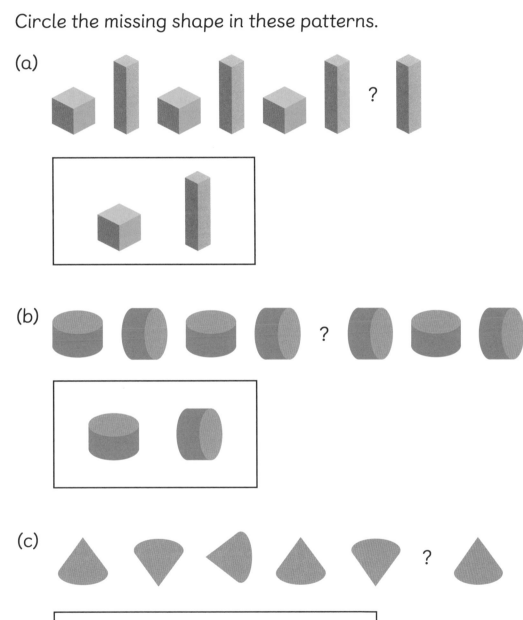

(b)

(c)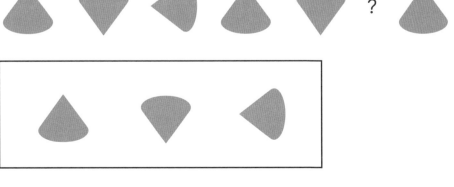

Review and challenge

1 Look at the shapes and complete the table.

Polygon	Name of polygon	Number of sides	Number of vertices

2 Sort the shapes.

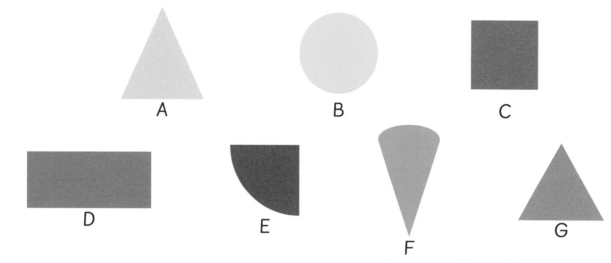

1 line of symmetry	More than 1 line of symmetry

3 Circle the figures that have a line of symmetry.

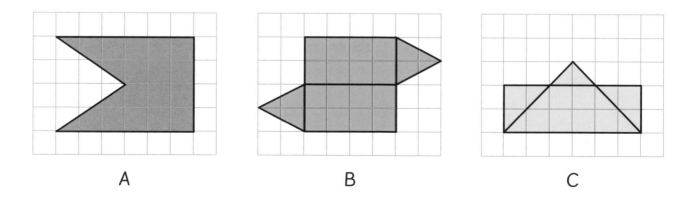

A   B   C

4 Copy these figures on the square grid paper below.

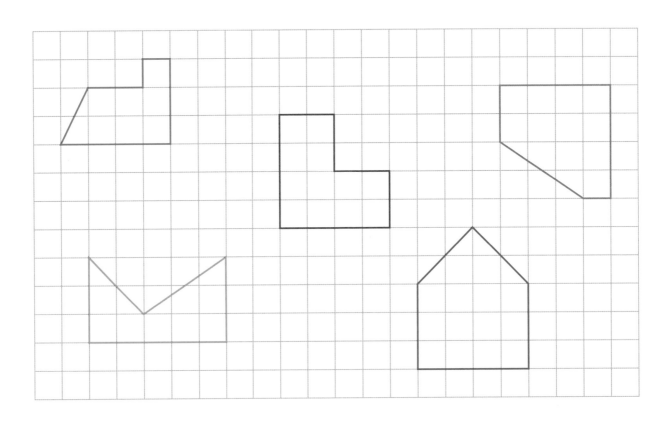

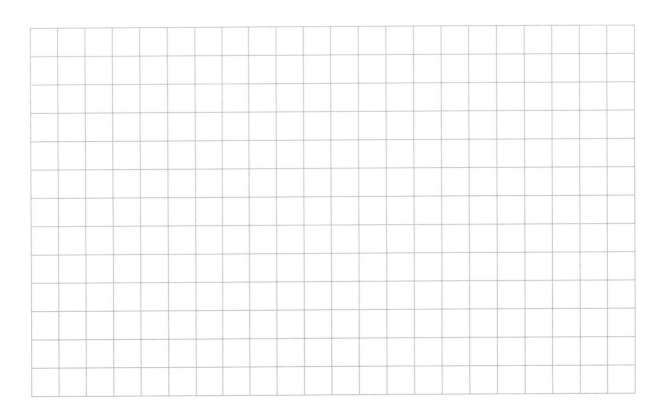

5 Circle the missing shape in these patterns.

(a)

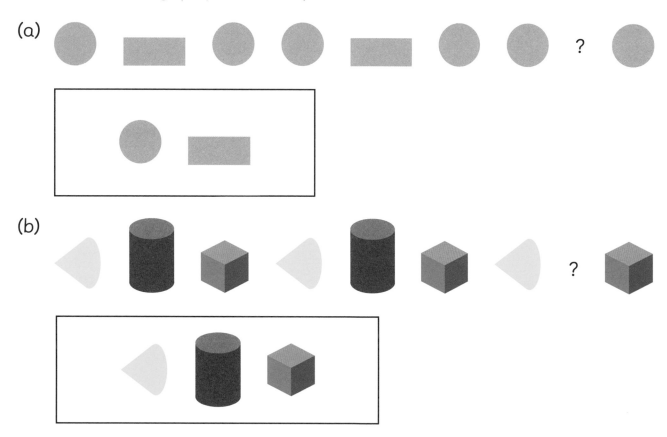

(b)

6 What is the 1st shape? Draw the shape in the space provided.

(a)

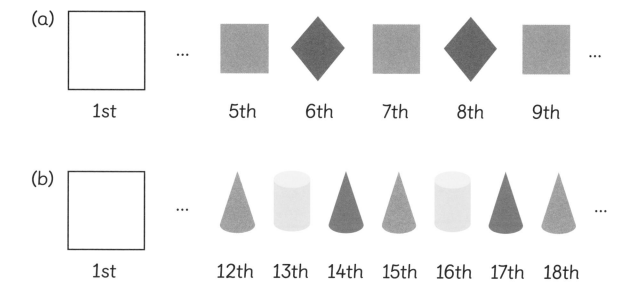

1st ... 5th 6th 7th 8th 9th ...

(b)

1st ... 12th 13th 14th 15th 16th 17th 18th ...

7 Circle the shape that does not belong in the group.

(a)

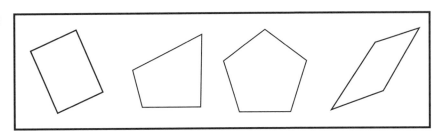

(b)

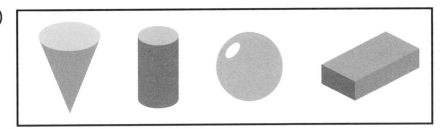

8 Name the 3D shapes made by folding these flat shapes.

(a)

(b)

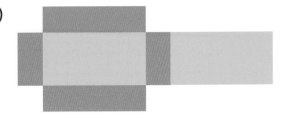

(c)

(d)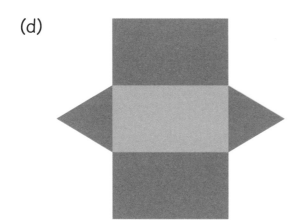

Answers

Page 5   **1 (a)** 4 sides **(b)** 4 sides **(c)** 3 sides **(d)** 3 sides

2

Page 7   **1** triangle 3, 3   **2** rectangle 4, 4   **3** heptagon 7, 7   **4** hexagon 6, 6   **5** pentagon 5, 5
         6 octagon 8, 8   **7** square 4, 4   **8** triangle 3, 3

Page 9   **1** tick   **2** tick   **3** tick   **4** cross   **5** cross   **6** cross   **7** tick   **8** tick

Page 11   **1** Answers will vary.   **2** Answers will vary.

3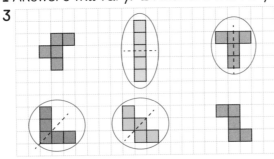

Page 13   **1** 3 vertices: C, E;   4 vertices: D, F, G, H;   5 vertices: A, B
         2 no line of symmetry: D, E;   one line of symmetry: A, B, C, F;   more than one line of
         symmetry: G, H

Page 15   **1** Shapes correctly copied. **2** Answers will vary.

Page 17   **1** Answers will vary. **2 (a)** ● **(b)** ▼ **(c)** ■

Page 19   **1 (a)** ■ **(b)** ● **2 (a)** ◗ **(b)** ■

         3 Answers will vary.

Page 21   **1**   **2**

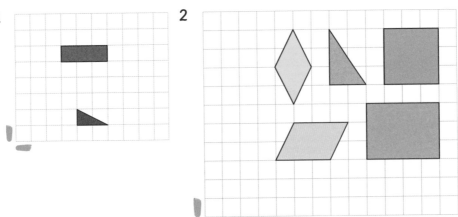

Page 23   1 (a) 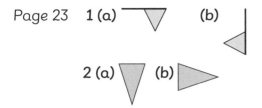   (b)

2 (a) 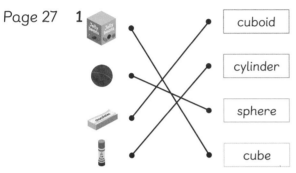   (b)

Page 25   **1** 4 people can have a piece of cake.
2 The clock will show 12:15.
3 The pizza will serve 5 friends.

Page 27   **1**

cuboid

cylinder

sphere

cube

2 Answers will vary. **3** Answers will vary.

Page 30   **1**

cuboid		
prism		
cube		
cylinder		
pyramid		
cone		

Page 31   **2** pyramid, 5 faces, 5 vertices, 8 edges; cuboid, 6 faces, 8 vertices, 12 edges; cube, 6 faces, 8 vertices, 12 edges; triangular prism, 5 faces, 6 vertices, 9 edges **3** Answers will vary.

Page 33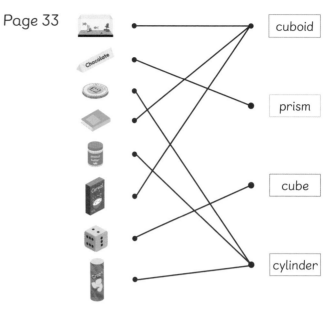

cuboid

prism

cube

cylinder

Page 35   **1** Answers will vary. **2** Answers will vary.

Page 37   **1**

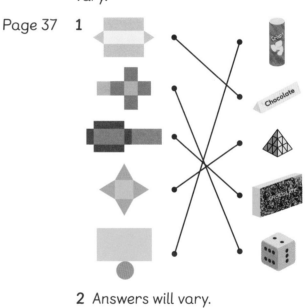

2 Answers will vary.

Page 38   **1 (a)**

Page 39   **(b)** medium cylinder

2 (a)   **(b)**   **(c)**

Page 40   **1** square, 4 sides, 4 vertices; rectangle, 4 sides, 4 vertices; triangle, 3 sides, 3 vertices; triangle, 3 sides, 3 vertices.

Answers continued

Page 41 **2** 1 line of symmetry: A, E, F; more than one line: B, C, D, G

3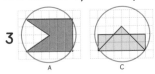

Page 42 **4** shapes correctly copied.

Page 43 **5 (a)** ▬ **(b)** ⬤ **6 (a)** ◼ **(b)** ⬜

Page 44 **7 (a)** ⬠ **(b)** ▬ **8 (a)** cube **(b)** cuboid

Page 45 **(c)** pyramid **(d)** triangular prism